BALL GAMES

by Jason Page

LOOK OUT!

The fastest baseball pitchers can throw the ball faster than 93 mph (150 km/h).

ANCIENT ORIGINS

From soccer to table tennis, softball to field hockey, the Olympic ball games are some of the most varied and exciting sports at the Games!

OLYMPIC HISTORY

Many of the ball games played at the modern Olympic Games have ancient origins. Field hockey is one of the oldest sports in the world, and this stone carving shows a hockey game in ancient Greece. Roman soldiers sometimes played soccer, only they used the heads of their enemies rather than a ball!

A field hockey game in ancient Greece

SUPER STATS

Here are the diameters of some of the balls used at the Games. You can see that they come in many different sizes!

Table tennis ball
1.5 inches (3.8 cm)
Field hockey ball
2.7 inches (7.0 cm)
Softball
3.9 inches (10 cm)
Soccer ball
8.6 inches (22 cm)
Basketball
9.4 inches (24 cm)

STRIKING GOLD

Modern Olympians are dedicated athletes who spend countless hours training in preparation for the Games. But at the first Olympics, things were rather different. In 1896, the first tennis gold medal was won by John Pius Boland (GBR), who went to the Games as a spectator and decided to compete at the last minute!

WATCH THIS SPACE

The ball games at the 2000 Olympics will take place in many Sydney venues—even famous Bondi Beach will get a slice of the action as the venue for the beach volleyball event.

As for soccer, the early rounds will take place in other cities (see page 27).

OLYMPICS FACT FILE

)) The Olympic Games were first held in Olympia, Greece, around 3,000 years ago. They took place every four years until they were abolished in A. D. 393.

)) A Frenchman named Pierre de Coubertin (1863–1937) revived the Games. The first modern Olympics were held in Athens, Greece, in 1896.

)) The modern Games have been held every four years since 1896, except in 1916, 1940, and 1944, because of war. Special 10th-anniversary Games took place in 1906.

)) The symbol of the Olympic Games is five interlocking colored rings. Together, they represent the five different continents from which athletes come to compete.

NEW SPORTS

Not all of the Olympic ball games have such an impressive history. Some, such as softball, are relatively new. Like several other games, softball was invented in the last century. However, softball will be a medal sport for just the second time at the Olympic Games in Sydney.

U.S. softball player

DID YOU KNOW?

The greatest victory (or worst defeat, depending on which team you support!) in a team handball match occurred in 1980, when Yugoslavia beat Kuwait 44–10.

The first team handball players were soccer players who took up the sport as a way of keeping fit during the "off season."

The ball used in women's matches is slightly smaller and lighter than the one used in men's games.

HANDBALL HISTORY

The ancient Romans and Greeks played a game that was very similar to team handball. The rules of the modern game were not drawn up until 1917. Team handball first appeared at the Olympic Games in 1936, when it was played outside with teams of 11 players. It reappeared as an indoor 7-player sport in 1972 and has been part of the Games ever since.

Goalkeeper restraining line: The goalkeeper is not allowed to cross this line when trying to make a save.

Goal area line: Only the goalkeeper is allowed inside the goal area, but attacking players may jump over the line and shoot while in midair.

Handball field

Seong-Ok Oh

WHAT A MATCH!

At left, Seong-Ok Oh (KOR) takes a flying shot at Denmark's goal during the women's final at the 1996 Olympics. The match was one of the closest and most exciting in the history of the Games. Denmark was awarded a penalty shot just before the final buzzer but a heroic save by the Korean goalkeeper kept the score tied. The match then went to overtime, and the Danes pulled off a stunning victory.

REIGNING OLYMPIC CHAMPIONS: Men: Croatia

TEAM HANDBALL

Team handball is based on the rules of soccer. The big difference is that you use your hands, not your feet, to control the ball!

Penalty line: Penalties are called against players who commit serious fouls. Penalty throws are taken from the penalty line, 23 feet (7m) in front of the goal.

Free throw line: If a defender commits a foul between this line and the goal area, the attackers are given a free throw from the edge of the dotted line.

RULE BOOK

The object is to score as many points as possible by throwing the ball into the opposition's goal. Players are allowed to hold the ball for three seconds or take three steps with it, before they must pass, shoot, or bounce it on the ground. Only the goalkeeper is allowed to touch the ball with his or her feet.

SPEEDOMETER

Handball is a fast and physical game. Players throw the ball through the air at speeds of up to 62 mph (100 km/h). That's how fast the fastest birds can fly!

TENNIS

Although tennis was included in the first modern Olympics in 1896, it was left out of the Games in 1928 and was not included again as a full medal sport until 1988.

WIMBLEDON WINNERS

A total of 29 Olympic gold medal winners have also won the Lawn Tennis Championships at Wimbledon — the most prestigious grand slam tennis tournament. Those double champions include Andre Agassi, the reigning Olympic champion, who won the men's singles at Wimbledon in 1992.

GOING TO GROUND

The tennis courts used at the Games in Sydney will have a high-tech, rubberized hard court surface that's designed to suit all playing styles.

LEARN THE LINGO

Ace: a winning serve that the other player fails to hit

Deuce: when both players have 40 points

Fault: a serve that falls outside the service lines. Players who serve two faults in a row lose the point

Let: this means the point must be played again

Love: zero points

REIGNING OLYMPIC CHAMPIONS: Men's singles: Andre Agassi (USA)

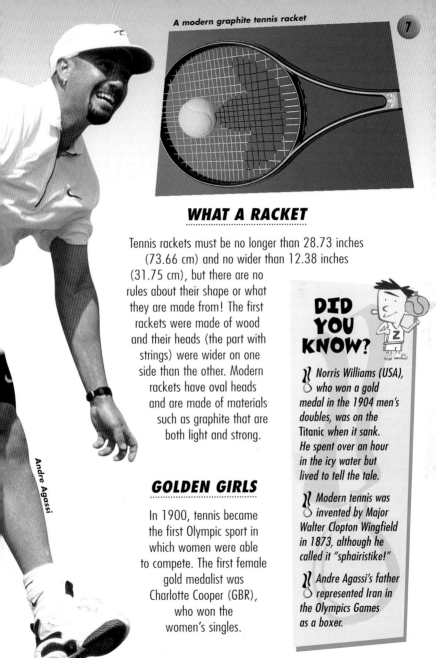

A modern graphite tennis racket

Andre Agassi

WHAT A RACKET

Tennis rackets must be no longer than 28.73 inches (73.66 cm) and no wider than 12.38 inches (31.75 cm), but there are no rules about their shape or what they are made from! The first rackets were made of wood and their heads (the part with strings) were wider on one side than the other. Modern rackets have oval heads and are made of materials such as graphite that are both light and strong.

GOLDEN GIRLS

In 1900, tennis became the first Olympic sport in which women were able to compete. The first female gold medalist was Charlotte Cooper (GBR), who won the women's singles.

DID YOU KNOW?

Norris Williams (USA), who won a gold medal in the 1904 men's doubles, was on the Titanic when it sank. He spent over an hour in the icy water but lived to tell the tale.

Modern tennis was invented by Major Walter Clopton Wingfield in 1873, although he called it "sphairistike!"

Andre Agassi's father represented Iran in the Olympics Games as a boxer.

WINNING COMBINATION

Dynamic duo Gigi Fernandez and Mary Joe Fernandez (USA) won the women's doubles in 1992, and they successfully defended their title in 1996. Despite sharing the same last name, the two players are not related. However, two brothers, Reggie and Laurie Doherty (GBR), did win the men's doubles in 1900.

Gigi Fernandez & Mary Joe Fernandez

The net must be 35.7 inches (91.4 cm) high in the center of the court.

A serve must land in the opponent's service area opposite the server.

Women's doubles, Wimbledon 1998

DID YOU KNOW?

Tennis balls at the Olympics are stored in a refrigerator until they are ready to be used. This ensures that they are all equally bouncy!

Players automatically lose a point if they touch the ball with their body or if they touch the net.

Until 1924, there was a "mixed doubles" event at the Olympics with a male and female player on each team.

The inner sidelines mark the edge in singles matches.

The base line marks the farthest edge of the court. A ball landing beyond this line (or the sidelines) on its first bounce is out.

TENNIS (CONTINUED)

Along with the singles events, there are also doubles events in which two players play as a team.

ON THE BALL

Tennis balls used in the Olympics must be 2.55–2.67 inches (6.54–6.85 cm) in diameter and weigh 1.98–2.05 ounces (56.7–58.5 g). When dropped from a height of 99 inches (254 cm) onto a concrete floor, they must bounce between 4.38–4.79 feet (134.62–147.32 cm).

NATIONAL BOUNDARIES

In the early modern Games, doubles teams were often made up of two players from different countries. At Sydney, all doubles partners must have the same nationality, and only one team is allowed per country.

In doubles matches, the outer sidelines are used to make the court wider.

SUPER STATS

Todd Woodbridge and Mark Woodforde (AUS) won the men's doubles at the 1996 Games. Neil Broad and Tim Henman (GBR) came in second.

Great Britain is on top of the medals' table in tennis with 16 gold medals. However, a British competitor hasn't won an Olympic tennis event since 1920! The United States is second with 14 golds, and France is third with eight.

BASKETBALL

Modern basketball was invented by an American, Dr. James Naismith in 1891, and the United States has dominated the sport ever since.

RACE AGAINST TIME

Michael Jordan →

Basketball players must play against the clock as well as their opponents. As soon as one team takes possession of the ball, that team has just 10 seconds to move into its opponent's half of the court and 30 seconds to try to score. Otherwise, the ball automatically goes to the other side.

SUPER STATS

The men's basketball event has been held 14 times at the Games, and the United States has won it 11 times. The women's event has been held six times, and the United States has notched three victories. The overall winners table is shown at left.

USA	14
Soviet Union/ Russia	5
Yugoslavia	1

Players may only run with the ball if they bounce it with one hand at every step. This is called dribbling. If a player stops moving, he or she cannot start dribbling again but must pass or shoot. Here, Michael Jordan (USA) shows how it's done during the 1992 final.

REIGNING OLYMPIC CHAMPIONS: Men: United States

WHAT'S THE SCORE?

When you watch a basketball game, you'll notice there's a wide, curved line around the basket at each end of the court. This is called the three-point arc. If players shoot the ball into the basket from beyond this line, they score three points. Scoring from in front of the line is worth only two points. The most spectacular way to score is to take a massive leap and thrust the ball into the basket from above. This is known as a slam dunk.

DID YOU KNOW?

Basketball made its first appearance at the modern Olympics in 1936. The medals were presented by Dr. James Naismith.

The basket must be fixed at exactly 10.01 feet (3.05 meters) above the ground.

The highest scoring game in Olympic history took place in 1988, when the men's team from Brazil beat China by 130–108!

DEADLY GAME

A game similar to modern basketball was first played by the Aztecs more than 500 years ago in Mexico. The aim was to get a ball made of rubber through a raised stone hoop (right). The Aztecs took their sport very seriously. At the end of a match, all the members of the losing team were put to death!

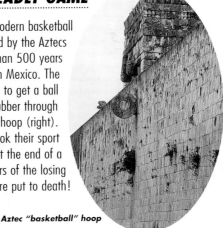

Aztec "basketball" hoop

VOLLEYBALL

There are two volleyball events at the Olympics: indoor volleyball and beach volleyball. First, we'll take a look at indoor volleyball.

ALL CHANGE

An indoor volleyball team is made up of six players—three at the front of the court and three at the back. Every time a team wins the right to serve, all the players on that team must change position, rotating clockwise around the court. The ball must be served by the player nearest the right-hand corner at the back of the court. This player must stand behind the baseline to hit the ball over the net.

LEARN THE LINGO

Attack zone: the front half of the court

Bump : a pass made using the forearm

Side out: when a team loses the right to serve

Spike: a hard hit from above the net

NICE TOUCH

Players are allowed to use any part of their bodies to control the ball, including their feet. However, once a player has touched the ball, that player may not touch it again until it has been hit by another player. A team is allowed to hit the ball no more than three times in a row. Players may not touch the net.

NEW RULES

Two new rules are being introduced to indoor volleyball in time for the 2000 Games. One is that players will score a point every time the ball lands on their opponents' side of the court — no matter who served the ball. The other new rule allows a special substitute player, called a "libero," to replace one of the players in the back row. Volleyball officials hope this will result in longer rallies!

Women's teams: United States vs. Ukraine, 1996

DID YOU KNOW?

⁇ Volleyball was invented in 1895 by William Morgan. He was a friend of Dr. James Naismith, the man who invented basketball.

⁇ Originally, Morgan called volleyball "mintonette," but no one knows why.

⁇ A line parallel to the net divides each half of the court across the middle. The three players at the back of the court are only allowed to spike the ball if they jump from behind this line.

ON THE ATTACK

1. The first stage in a classic volleyball attack is for one player to pass the ball to a teammate near the net.

2. This player sets the ball by tossing it up into the air.

3. A third player then completes the play, leaping above the net and smashing the ball down into the opponents' court. This move is known as a spike.

DID YOU KNOW?

? Beach volleyball was invented in California in the 1920s.

? The volleyball net is slightly higher in the men's competitions. The net is 7.97 feet (2.43 meters) high for men and 7.35 feet (2.24 meters) high for women.

? In beach volleyball, blocking an opponent's shot counts as one of your team's three hits of the ball. This rule doesn't apply indoors.

SAME DIFFERENCE?

As in indoor volleyball, each team may hit the ball no more than three times in a row. Each time players handle the ball, they must either pass it to their teammate or hit it over the net. However, the scoring system for beach volleyball is slightly different than for indoor volleyball. Only the team that served the ball at the start of the rally can win a point. If the serving team loses the rally, the other team gets to serve.

Karch Kiraly

Jackie Silva & Sandra Pires

Jackie Silva and Sandra Pires (BRA) kiss their gold medals after winning in women's beach volleyball at the 1996 Olympics.

VOLLEYBALL
(CONTINUED)

Beach volleyball made its first appearance at the Games in 1996, when it proved to be one of the most popular events.

TWO'S COMPANY

Beach volleyball is a game for just two players. This picture shows the reigning men's champions, Karch Kiraly and Kent Steffes (USA). Kiraly is widely regarded as the world's greatest volleyball player. He also won two gold medals in the indoor volleyball event at the 1984 and 1988 Games.

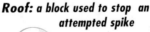

LEARN THE LINGO

Assist: passing the ball to a player for a kill

Dig: saving a low ball and hitting it back up into the air

Kill: any attacking shot that is unreturnable

Roof: a block used to stop an attempted spike

LIFE'S A BEACH

The dimensions of a beach volleyball court are identical to an indoor volleyball court, including the height of the net. The only difference is the surface. The outdoor game is played on a beach! Because the wind and sun can make a big difference to a game, players are required to change sides every five points.

YOU'RE OUT!

DID YOU KNOW?

Members of the batting side who get on base are allowed to steal other bases by sprinting to the next base when the fielders aren't looking.

The longest throw by a fielder in a baseball game measured 445.8 feet (135.9 meters)!

If the ball thrown by the pitcher hits the batter, the batter is allowed to walk to the next base, unopposed.

There are many ways to get a batter out. Here are three:

1. The batter is automatically out if he hits the ball and a fielder catches the ball before it lands.

2. The batter is out on strikes if he fails to hit the ball after the pitcher throws three strikes.

3. The batter is out if a fielder touches him with the ball while he is running from one base to another, or if a fielder with the ball gets to the base before him.

The Bases

1: first base
2: second base
3: third base
4: home plate

6: The area inside this square is known as the infield.

5: Pitcher's mound is a mound of earth 16 inches (40 cm) high where the player who throws the ball to the batter stands.

7: Foul lines. The batter must hit the ball between these two lines in order to reach base.

Outfield

BASEBALL

Baseball became a full Olympic sport in 1992, and Cuba won the gold medal. The Cuban team successfully defended its title at the 1996 Games and will be going for its third gold medal in a row at the Sydney Olympics.

Antonio Scull (CUB)

WHAT'S THE BIG IDEA?

Only men compete in Olympic baseball games. Players score points by hitting the ball, then running from one base to the next, until they return to home plate — where they started. Teams are made up of nine players. The teams take turns batting and fielding. Every time the team in the field gets three of its opponents out, that team gets to bat. Both teams get nine times at bat. The team with the most runs is the winner. If the score is tied, the teams play extra innings.

SPEEDOMETER

The fastest baseball pitchers can throw the ball more than 93 mph (150 km/h). That's faster than a family car going at top speed!

ESSENTIAL EQUIPMENT

Baseball bats are made of wood or aluminum and have smooth, rounded sides. The ball is about the same size as a tennis ball but much harder. It's made of cork or rubber with a leather skin. Batters wear plastic helmets to protect their heads, while players on the fielding side use large leather gloves to catch, or field, the ball.

SOFTBALL

Eight women's teams will compete in the softball tournament at the Sydney Games: Australia, Italy, Canada, New Zealand, Cuba, Japan, China, and the United States.

A hard plastic helmet protects the player's head

Catching mitt

Chest protector

SPOT THE DIFFERENCE

Softball was invented as an indoor version of baseball but there are some important differences:

1. Only women play softball at Olympic level. Men play baseball.

2. The ball used in softball is larger than in baseball, but the field is smaller.

3. In softball, the pitcher throws the ball underhand. Pitches are thrown overhand in baseball.

4. Softball players are not allowed to steal a base until the pitcher throws the ball. Baseball players can steal any time.

5. In softball, each side gets seven turns at bat (innings). There are nine innings in a baseball game.

SPEEDOMETER

The fastest softball pitch recorded at the last Games shot through the air at more than 73 mph (118 km/h). That's faster than a sailfish, the speediest creature on Earth.

NOT SO SOFT

There's nothing soft about softball! In fact, the person batting actually needs faster reactions than a baseball batter. Although the ball isn't pitched quite as fast as it is in baseball, the pitcher stands much closer to home plate — which means the batter has less time to react!

Face guard

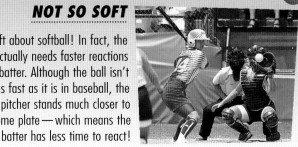

The catcher crouches behind the batter. The catcher's job is to catch the pitches that the batter misses. The catcher also must defend home plate. She needs to wear plenty of protective equipment, as this picture shows.

AMERICAN ALL-STARS

The U. S. softball team once played 106 games over nine years without losing a match. This phenomenal winning streak came to a temporary end when the Americans lost to China in 1995. However, a year later, at the 1996 Olympic Games, the U. S. team won the first softball gold medal.

Knee and shin pads

DID YOU KNOW?

Three-sided bats are allowed in softball but most teams prefer to use rounded bats like those used in baseball.

Softball is the most popular participation sport in the United States and is played by more than 20 million people worldwide.

Softball was originally called "kitten-ball" and "mush-ball!"

SILVER: China **BRONZE:** Australia

DID YOU KNOW?

 Table tennis has been known by many names, including gossima, whiff-whaff, flim-flam, and ping-pong.

 More people play table tennis than any other sport in the world. There are more than 40 million competitive players, plus those who just play for fun!

 In table tennis, players are not allowed to hit the ball until it has bounced on the table in front of them.

Table tennis bats can be any size or shape as long as 85 percent of the bat is wood. Each side of a bat is covered with a pimpled rubber surface no thicker than 0.08 inches (2 mm) or a layer of spongy foam faced with pimpled rubber no thicker than 0.16 inches (4 mm). These outer coats enable the players to hit the ball much faster.

The reigning men's Olympic champion, Liu Guoliang (CHN)

Deng Yaping

GET A GRIP

The reigning women's Olympic champion, Deng Yaping (CHN) holds the bat with an unusual grip called the "shake hands" grip. Most players (especially other Chinese players) use a grip called the "pen hold" grip.

TABLE TENNIS

Table tennis made its first appearance at the Games in 1988. Since then, it has proven that you don't need a big bat to be a big hit!

HISTORY LESSON

Table tennis was invented during the late 1800s and soon became a popular after-dinner game. At first, players used a ball carved from a champagne cork and cigar box lids for bats. By the early 1900s, toy companies had started making bats and balls.

SUPER STATS

China has won more gold medals in the table tennis events than any other nation with a grand total of nine. In second place is South Korea with two. Sweden is third with one.

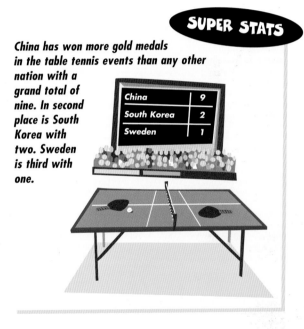

China	9
South Korea	2
Sweden	1

WHAT'S THE POINT?

Players win a point every time they hit a valid shot that their opponent can't return. The winner is the first player to reach 21 points, but players must beat their opponent by at least two points. So, if one player has 21 points and the other has 20, the first player still needs another point to win.

Women's singles: Deng Yaping (CHN)

TABLE TENNIS
(CONTINUED)

*J*ust like lawn tennis, table tennis also has a doubles
tournament in which two players play together.

*Each
table
tennis match
at the Olympics
is watched by
an umpire who sits
on a raised chair in
line with the net.
This gives him or
her a bird's-eye
view. Other
judges watch
for
faults.*

Table tennis doubles

SPEEDOMETER

LT88

**Despite its small size, a table tennis
ball whizzes across the table at speeds
of up to 105 mph (170 km/h). That's
faster than a small plane can travel!**

AT YOUR SERVICE

When serving in table tennis,
players must throw the ball at
least 6 inches (16 cm) into the
air and hit it as it falls. Their
shot must also bounce on both
sides of the net. In singles
matches, players are allowed to
serve to and from any part of
the table. In doubles, the ball
must be hit diagonally across the
table from one right-hand
corner to the other.

SKILLS & SHOTS

Table tennis requires lightning reactions and great coordination. Players need to master a number of different shots, including slices — which make the ball spin off at unexpected angles — and smashes — which wallop the ball down onto the opponents' side of the table with great force.

DID YOU KNOW?

♫ Table tennis balls must be orange or white. They weigh just 0.09 ounces (2.5 g). That's 8 times lighter than a golf ball!

♫ China won 7 of the 8 golds awarded in table tennis at the last two Olympics.

♫ Certain glues used to make table tennis bats are banned at the Games because they can make the ball travel 19 mph (30 km/h) faster than ordinary glues!

TAKING TURNS

In doubles games, the players must hit the ball in a strict order. The server hits it to the receiver, who hits it to the server's partner, who then hits it to the receiver's partner, who hits it back to the server. If a player hits the ball out of turn, the team loses the point.

Kong Linghui

Women's doubles: Deng Yaping and Qiao Hong (CHN)

FIELD HOCKEY STICKS

Tycho van Meer (NED)
& Jaime Amat (ESP)

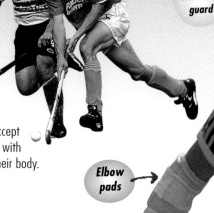

Field hockey is a bit like soccer. The aim is to score goals by hitting the ball into the other team's goal. Field hockey sticks are shaped like long hooks. Their curved ends are flat on one side and rounded on the other. Players may only hit the ball with the flat side of their stick and, except for the goalie, may not touch the ball with any part of their body.

Helmet with face guard

Elbow pads

DID YOU KNOW?

The term "hockey" is thought to come from the French word "hoquet," which means a shepherd's crook, because of its curved shape.

Field hockey is played on a field 100 yards (91.4 meters) long and 60 yards (55 meters) wide, which is slightly smaller than a soccer field. Each team has 11 players.

Four different Indian players, all named Balbir Singh, have won medals in men's field hockey at the Olympics.

The goalkeeper is allowed to throw or kick the ball, as well as hit it with the hockey stick.

ANCIENT ORIGINS

Field hockey is one of the oldest known sports. It was played in Egypt more than 1,000 years before the first Olympic Games were held in ancient Greece. The modern rules of field hockey were drawn up in 1886. The men's field hockey event was held for the first time at the modern Olympics in 1908.

Large pads protect the goalkeeper's legs

FIELD HOCKEY

Field hockey may be more ancient than the Olympic Games, but it's been brought up-to-date with an exciting new rule!

The goalkeeper is allowed to use any body part to block a shot.

WHAT'S NEW?

A new rule, which will be introduced for the first time at the Games in Sydney, says that attacking players can no longer be offside — meaning that players can now score from any position on the field. The purpose of this new rule is to encourage more goals.

SUPER STATS

India has won eight gold medals in the field hockey events — more than any other country. It won every single final from 1928 to 1956. Tied for second place are Great Britain and Pakistan with three golds each. The Netherlands and Australia are tied for third with two.

SOCCER

Soccer will be the first sport to be played at the Olympic Games in Sydney. In fact, the first game will kick off before the opening ceremony!

The Nigerian team is all smiles after defeating Argentina in the soccer final at the 1996 Games. It was the first time that a team from Africa had won the event.

LEARN THE LINGO

Red card: if a player commits a serious offense, he or she is shown a red card and sent off the field by the referee

Striker: an attacking player

Sweeper: a defensive player whose job is to clear the ball away from the goal

Winger: a player who plays down the sides of the field

The Nigerian soccer team

BANNED!

Soccer is the only Olympic sport ever to have been banned by royal decree. In the thirteenth century, King Edward II outlawed soccer in England because he was afraid that his subjects were spending too much time kicking around a ball when they should have been practicing their archery skills. However, no one took much notice of the King, and 800 years later, soccer has become the world's favorite sport!

KICKING OFF

At the 2000 Games, 16 men's teams and 8 women's teams will take part in the soccer competition. Professional players can participate in the men's competition but teams are only allowed to have three players who are over 23 years old. The women's competition, first held in 1996, is open to players over age 16.

DID YOU KNOW?

The United States women's team is the reigning world champion and is the favorite to win the gold medal in Sydney.

Danish center forward Sophus Nielsen scored 10 goals in 1908, when Denmark defeated France 17–1.

Soccer and water polo were the first team sports to be introduced to the modern Olympic Games. They became part of the Games in 1900.

GOING WALKABOUT

Brisbane ●
Sydney ●
Canberra ●
Melbourne ●

Soccer is the only Olympic sport in which some events will be held outside of Sydney. Although the finals will take place at the Sydney Football Stadium, the elimination rounds will be held in the cities of Melbourne, Canberra, and Brisbane.

DID YOU KNOW?

♫ Badminton players sometimes run as much as 4 miles (6 km) during a match.

♫ In Sydney, 172 athletes will compete in badminton.

♫ Badminton made its Olympic debut in 1992.

GAME & MATCH

In badminton, the first person or team to win two games wins the match. To win a game in the women's singles, players need at least 11 points. The minimum required in all other events is 15 points.

HOW TO SERVE

Players serve by dropping the shuttle and hitting it as it falls. They may only serve underarm while standing still with both feet on the ground, and the shuttle must be struck below the waist. In badminton, only the player who serves can win a point.

THE ONE THAT GOT AWAY

Asian countries lead the world when it comes to badminton. China, Indonesia, Malaysia, and South Korea won 14 out of the 15 medals at the 1996 Games. The exception was the men's singles gold medalist, Poul-Erik Hoyer-Larsen (DEN).

Poul-Erik Hoyer-Larsen (DEN)

BADMINTON

Badminton is like a ball game —without the ball! It first appeared at the Olympic Games in 1992.

FEATHER POWER

Badminton isn't really a ball game. Badminton is played with a super-speedy missile made from cork and goose feathers, called a shuttlecock, or shuttle, for short. The aim is to score points by hitting the shuttle over the net so that it lands in the opponent's service court.

LEARN THE LINGO

Drive:
an attacking shot played from the center of the court

Drop shot:
a low power shot that just clears the net, then falls to the ground

Lob:
a high shot that goes over the opponent's head and lands at the back of the court

Round the head:
a forehand shot played over the top of the head

Camilla Martin (DEN) retrieves a drop shot.

BADMINTON
(CONTINUED)

Badminton is one of the few sports at the Olympics in which men and women compete together.

Along with the men's and women's doubles events, there's also a mixed doubles event at the Olympics.

SPEEDOMETER

Believe it or not, badminton is the world's fastest racket sport. The shuttlecock can reach speeds of 161 mph (260 km/h) — the average racing speed of a Formula One car!

A WINNING TEAM

The key to success in doubles events is good communication between teammates. Usually, each player has different responsibilities. In mixed doubles, for example, the female player usually stays close to the net while the male player runs around the back of the court, chasing deep shots.

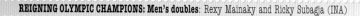

REIGNING OLYMPIC CHAMPIONS: Men's doubles: Rexy Mainaky and Ricky Subagja (INA)

Badminton mixed doubles

PLAY AREA

On a badminton court, you'll see two sidelines and two baselines. In a doubles game, the outer lines are the play area, except when serving. Then, only the inner baseline counts. In a singles game, the reverse is true. The inner lines are the play area, except when serving. Then, the outer baseline counts as part of the court.

DID YOU KNOW?

The 16 feathers used on each shuttlecock come from three different geese!

The net is set at the same height in all the badminton events: 5.1 feet (155 cm) at the post and 5 feet (152.4 cm) in the middle.

Malaysia won its first Olympic medal in 1992 when two brothers, Razif and Jalani Sidek, took the bronze in the men's doubles.

WHAT'S IN A NAME?

A game very similar to modern badminton became popular in India in the 1800s. It was called "poona," and it was introduced into Great Britain by an English aristocrat, the Duke of Beaufort. The Duke played a version of poona at his home, Badminton House in Gloucestershire. The name of the house soon became the name of the game as well!

Duke of Beaufort

INDEX

Acknowledgments
We would like to thank Ian Hodge, Rosalind Beckman, Jackie Gaff, and Elizabeth Wiggans for their assistance. Cartoons by John Alston.
Copyright © 2000 *ticktock* Publishing Ltd. Printed in Hong Kong.
First published in Great Britain by ticktock Publishing Ltd., The Offices in the Square, Hadlow, Tonbridge, Kent TN11 0DD, Great Britain.
Picture Credits: AKG photo: 2–3t, 11br; Allsport: OFC, 3bl, 4bl, 4–5c, 6–7c, 7tr, 8tl, 8–9c, 10–11c, 12–13 (main pic), 14bl, 14–15c, 16–17c, 18–19c, 19tr, 20bl, 20–21c, 22–23t, 23br, 24tr, 24–25 (main pic), 26–27c, 28bl, 28–29 (main pic), 30–31c; Ann Ronan @ Image Select: 31br; Empics: IFC. Picture research by Image Select.
Library of Congress Cataloging-in-Publishing Data
Page, Jason.
  Ball games : soccer, table tennis, team handball, field hockey, badminton, and lots, lots more / by Jason Page.
    p. cm. -- (Zeke's Olympic pocket guide)
Includes index.
Summary: Describes the ball games of the Olympic Games and previews the athletic competition at the 2000 Summer Olympics in Sydney, Australia.
  ISBN 0-8225-5057-1 (pbk. : alk. paper)
1. Ball games--Juvenile literature. 2. Olympics--Juvenile literature. [1. Ball games. 2. Olympics.] I. Title. II. Series.
  GV861 .P24 2000
  796.3--dc21
                                                                                        00-008096